SEO

The Essential Guide

Stephanie Clarke

SEO – The Essential Guide is also available in accessible formats for people with any degree of visual impairment. The large print edition and e-book (with accessibility features enabled) are available from Need2Know. Please let us know if there are any special features you require and we will do our best to accommodate your needs.

First published in Great Britain in 2012 by
Need2Know
Remus House
Coltsfoot Drive
Peterborough
PE2 9BF
Telephone 01733 898103
Fax 01733 313524
www.need2knowbooks.co.uk

Contents

Introduction

As the world becomes increasingly reliant on the Internet to provide general information and knowledge as well as to market and sell goods and services, search engine optimization has become a vital part of Internet success. The Internet gives users access to billions upon billions of websites and pages, and the question is no longer if the information can be found, but rather what source of information is the best, most reliable, or most easily accessed and viewed. It is this second aspect of Internet use that has created the need for search engine optimization, otherwise referred to as SEO.

When a user begins their Internet experience, it often starts with the utilisation of a search engine, the most common one being Google, followed by Yahoo! and Bing. As they type in their search query, these engines to go to work locating and displaying the most accurate and relevant results. It has been found that the search results which are found and displayed on the first page are the most likely to be clicked on and visited, and this is where the importance of SEO can be seen.

With this information in hand, many websites and businesses have realised how important it is to be listed at the top of the search results to increase visibility and site visitor traffic. The problem now became how website managers could go about creating sites that are easily recognised and ranked highly by search engines. This is where the importance of search engine optimization came into the spotlight, and has since become a major aspect of any successful Internet marketing campaign.

Search engine optimization focuses on creating a website that will be able to be seen more frequently and easily by Internet users who utilise search engines to locate sites and information. It is a multidimensional process which can start all the way from the creation of the site through to how both users and search engines can navigate the links within the site. Creating a website that functions well with search engine optimization will have a number of necessary aspects taken into consideration.

'It has been found that the search results which are found and displayed on the first page are the most likely to be clicked on and visited, and this is where the importance of SEO can be seen.'

We will look into all the different aspects of search engine optimization and the steps that you need to take in order to create a high-quality website with optimized search results. It is important when creating a website that is geared to high SEO results, that you start with the necessary research before actually implementing the methods. We will go over the types of research that you need to do and the importance of learning from the information you gather.

Some of the areas that are necessary to research before starting your SEO strategy include learning and knowing your target audience. What this means is identifying and researching the trends of the audience that you want to read your website, or purchase your product or service. This is the first and arguably the most important part of creating a high-quality SEO strategy from the ground up. Your target audience has the key information necessary to create an SEO plan with high-quality and high-potential keywords and phrases that can make your website stand out from other sites.

This easy-to-read and informative book is written for those who are looking to learn more about search engine optimization and begin to implement strategies to increase their SEO effectiveness and website visibility. The information about search engine optimization that is covered within this book can help both new and experienced website publishers to create or enhance the visibility of their website as well as increase the amount of website traffic.

We will cover a variety of topics that directly relate to effective search engine optimization. Some of the topics include keyword research, link building, content management, site usability, as well as looking into just how search engines go about ranking and valuing the relevance of websites within a certain industry or category.

It is important to first understand how search engines operate and how they decide upon which sites to display as results before you are able to create a website to cater to that information. The research that is done before the start of your SEO campaign is necessary in order to learn how to best take advantage of the information. Throughout this book you will learn how search engines work, and how search engine optimization can help your business or website become more visible to the everyday Internet user.

Throughout the guide we will accompany the information with an example as a way to better help you understand and visualise how to optimize your search results. This will give you a chance to see how to optimize your HTML as well as provide examples so that you can better grasp the concepts behind high-quality SEO websites. For our example website we will be using a fitness information site offering exercise ideas, workouts and at-home videos for sale.

We will walk through each step that we explain and how we would apply it to the example website, www.tonyasfitnessonline.com.

Chapter One

What is Search Engine Optimization?

Definition

Search engine optimization, commonly referred to as 'SEO', can be defined as the process used to increase the visibility of a page within search results, through a number of different techniques, strategies and steps. SEO includes a variety of methods aimed at increasing the 'organic', or unpaid, search results on search engines as well as increasing the page ranking as seen in search results.

Search engine optimization focuses on creating a website that will come up at the top of the search results for a number of specific search queries. This is accomplished through a variety of methods including quality content, proper use of HTML, keyword research, understanding the basics of search engines, as well as site promotion and link building.

Basics of search engine optimization

Search engine optimization is comprised of a number of small steps or processes that lead to the creation of a website that ranks high in search results. It is important to realise that SEO is a collaboration of a number of smaller aspects and when they work together can help to increase site visibility and page rankings.

'Search engine optimization, commonly referred to as 'SEO', can be defined as the process used to increase the visibility of a page within search results, through a number of different techniques, strategies and steps.'

Some of the most important basics of SEO include:

- Understanding search engines.
- Keyword research and development.
- Site design and usability.
- Site content.
- Link building and link popularity.

In order to successfully accomplish search engine optimization it is important to research all of the different aspects and methods. The most success comes when each of these parts are used in a collaborative effort, with each providing support for the other.

'There are four major functions of a search engine and they are: building an index, crawling, determining relevancy and page rankings, and then presenting the results to the user.'

How do search engines operate?

It is difficult to contemplate just how search engines are able to take any number of search queries that are entered and return with a number of relevant results. In the matter of a couple of seconds an Internet user is provided with the most relevant results to the search terms that he or she entered. Learning just how the search engines come up with this information is an important step in being able to understand and master search engine optimization.

The Internet is filled with billions of websites and pages, and each time a search query is made, the search engines go through all of these pages and make connections with what they deem are the most relevant and valued results. There are four major functions of a search engine and they are: building an index, crawling, determining relevancy and page rankings, and then presenting the results to the user.

Crawling and indexing

Crawling refers to the process which search engines go through in order to create an index, of web pages and links. These software bots search through available websites and index the information on the site as well as links that are available to and from the site. Through the information gathered through this process, search engines begin to create and build an index of sites that are visited and the content of those sites.

It is the indexes that are built through the crawling process which are accessed and searched when trying to determine the search results on a specific search query. Search engines use automated robots to create their indexes of websites, pages and links, which are then stored in extremely large databases around the world. Many search engines will have their indexes updated on a regular basis, whether that is monthly or weekly or periodically as needed. These bots will locate all links stemming from a web page as well as the links that connect to that page.

Determining relevancy and page rankings

Each time a search term or phrase is entered into a search engine, the software searches through their indexes in order to produce the most relevant and reliable list of results. Search engine software has been developed to judge all of the web pages within their indexes in a way that will produce a list that is determined both by the relevancy of the site to the search query as well as the overall value and reliability of the information on the site.

When search engines were first created and used, the formula for determining relevancy was rather simple and focused mostly on the most displayed words on a site or page in order to rank search results. As the Internet has become more complex, search engines now rely on a number of different factors in order to compute the relevancy of web pages to a search query. Modern search engines no longer simply look at the text on the page, but also take into consideration a number of other factors including page titles, the links within your site, onsite links to other sites, as well as links to your site from other sites.

Why is SEO important for website success?

Search engine optimization is an important part of Internet marketing and overall website success for a number of reasons. First and foremost it is the way to separate your business or website from the millions of others with similar information, products or services. Each and every search query will come back with thousands of results for users to navigate through. Without implementing an SEO strategy, your website is not likely to be ranked towards the top of the results and therefore is less likely to gain organic traffic from search engine queries, which are the most used methods of locating information online.

In order to drive enough traffic to your website to make it successful you need to have enough visibility in order to make that possible. Properly utilised search engine optimization will provide your business or website with the visibility necessary to help improve website traffic as well as sales or revenue.

'Properly utilised search engine optimization will provide your business or website with the visibility necessary to help improve website traffic as well as sales or revenue.'

Summing Up

- Search engine optimization is the process of getting a website listed higher within the search rankings for certain keywords and phrases through a variety of methods.

- The main aspects of search engine optimization include understanding how search engines operate, site design, site content, keyword research and link building.

- Search engines operate by first crawling through websites in order to discover information contained and then indexing this information for quick access when search queries are made.

- Search engines use a number of methods in order to determine the relevancy and page rankings of websites connected to a specific search term or phrase with the goal of best answering the user's question.

- SEO is an important part of website success because it focuses on increasing visibility of the website as well as overall search ranking which increases website traffic.

Chapter Two

Keyword Research

Definition

Keyword research can be defined as the practice of discovering what keywords Internet users of a target audience use when searching for information online. It is utilised by search engine optimization marketers when trying to find the exact search terms that are used by people on a variety of search engines. Keyword research has become an important part of Internet marketing and especially influential within the search engine optimization field.

Importance of keyword research

The beginning of any successful campaign is based around the research needed to make the campaign successful. When it comes to SEO campaigns, keyword research is the first, and possible most important, aspect to creating an SEO plan that will yield good results. Almost every other part of your campaign will be based around the information that is gained through your keyword research.

Keyword research is an extremely important aspect of search engine optimization and search engine marketing. It is this research that can enable you to better understand your target audience and can lead you to gaining higher return activities within the search engine optimization field. While the goal of keyword research is to learn more about the terms used to search the Internet, the knowledge that you gain supplies you with much more information than just that.

Keyword research gives you an opportunity to take a look at your customer base and learn more about what makes them tick, and what interests them. Being able to learn more about your customer base as a whole is a great way

'It is this research that can enable you to better understand your target audience and can lead you to gaining higher return activities within the search engine optimization field.'

to better target your website, business and overall Internet marketing as well as search engine optimization. The importance of keyword research goes far beyond grasping more knowledge about your audience and can provide you with a wide variety of information about general demand.

Being able to know what the everyday and common Internet user is searching for on the Internet allows you to gain a vast knowledge that can help in any business situation. Keyword research provides you with information to depict shifts in the demand for certain products or services, and can help your business to better prepare and respond to the constantly changing conditions of the market.

Keyword research gives you the ability to gain access to the knowledge within customers, what drives them and what the motivation behind their searches actually is. The most important part of this research is that it can be applied to any imaginable niche market currently out there. The usefulness of keyword research will only grow with the nation's dependency on the Internet and use of search engines.

What are the steps of keyword research?

There are four main steps when it comes to performing keyword research. Following these steps will help you to create a strong keyword presence on your site.

Research your audience

The first step to researching possible keywords for your site, is to start by looking at the audience, or audiences, that you are targeting, or marketing your site to. Recognising and learning about your target audience is the first step in any Internet marketing campaign, and is essential to learning the right keywords needed to reach this audience. Through the research conducted about your target audience, you will be better able to choose keywords that they are currently, and will continue, searching for on a regular basis.

Example site: **Tonya's Fitness Online**

Who will we target?

- Working women.
- College females.
- Stay-at-home mums.
- Ages 18-35.

Consider:

- What is their Internet use?
- What are their outside interests?
- Popular demographic topics, websites?

Create your keyword list

After you have recognised who your target audience is, the next step is figuring out what keywords will best relate to your audience and how they will impact the rest of your SEO plan. Create a set of 10-20 keywords and phrases that you want to aim your site and strategy on. They should be based on the information you have gained through audience research. Keywords are the foundation of an SEO campaign or strategy, and can help you create an SEO optimized site from the page names to the link architecture. Having them laid out in front of you when you are designing the structure of the site is a good way to keep your keyword use constant and optimized.

'After you have recognised who your target audience is, the next step is figuring out what keywords will best relate to your audience and how they will impact the rest of your SEO plan.'

Example site: **Tonya's Fitness Online**

Keyphrases we will target:

- Get rid of belly fat.
- Bikini season.
- Losing baby weight.
- Flat abs.
- At-home exercises.

Analyse your competition

When you have put together your overall SEO strategy with your keywords in mind, it is important to look at the industry you are targeting and their keyword usage. You can do this through a number of programs, which we will discuss later, that can help provide you with data and analysis. By looking at the other websites within your topic area it will allow you to see other keywords that are being used, their popularity and what kind of results they are yielding. Doing research on your industry can help you to think of alternate keywords and phrases that you had initially not been thinking about targeting.

Example Site: **Tonya's Fitness Online**

What to analyse?

- Popular fitness sites.
- Popular online weight loss programs.
- Popular fitness blogs and advice columns.

Keyword query

Once you have established what your main keywords are going to be, it is important to test their popularity. This can be done through a keyword research tool, many of which are available for free. Many of these tools will also export the results into an Excel document for you, that way you can easily identify your main keywords and your tail keywords. These results help you to see what keywords will be most effective, how to organise them and can make copy writing and link building easier.

Example Site: **Tonya's Fitness Online**

How do our keywords stack up?

▨ What is the popularity of each term?

▨ Will we be able to compete against others?

Will it target our core audience?

What's the value of a keyword?

While it is relatively easy to learn and determine which keywords will best translate into high SEO factors as well as page visits, it is more difficult to determine just how valuable that keyword actually is. There are a number of different factors to consider when trying to determine how valuable a keyword is to your business, website or organisation. Before even trying to determine the value of the keyword or phrase it is important to consider the following questions:

▨ Is it relevant to your web page and what you offer?

▨ Will Internet users find what they are searching for on your website through this keyword?

▨ Will the resulting traffic from this keyword help achieve financial or other goals for your website?

If, after considering these questions, it is clear that the keyword in question will work the best for your organisation or business, determining the actual value of the word will take some more investigation. One simple way to consider the value of a keyword is by actually using it in a search engine and looking at the results. Typically, when there are a lot of paid advertising results, found at the top and to the right-hand side of the regular results, it suggests that it is a popular keyword, and therefore may hold more value to you or your organisation.

Keyword popularity

Determining the popularity of a keyword is an important part of devising a search engine optimization campaign. The popularity of a keyword is determined by the amount of times that specific word or phrase is used in a search engine capacity. Each and every time that an Internet user types in a keyword or phrase into a search engine it is recorded and catalogued within the engine's indexes and databases.

Trying to pinpoint the exact popularity and resulting traffic from one specific keyword is an almost impossible task to achieve. This is simply because the amount of searches for any one keyword is a volatile activity whose change is subject to any number of reasons. However, what can be done to correctly discover the most popular keywords is to pin them against other varieties of the keyword, such as the plural versus the singular, and determine which option translates to the highest amount of traffic results. For example, the term 'diary' may yield much larger traffic results than the plural form 'diaries'.

Keyword research services

In order to properly determine the popularity of a keyword, there are a number of different services available online to help provide you with the necessary information. Some of the more popular services that are available to provide you with necessary keyword popularity information include:

- Wordtracker's Free Basic Keyword Demand.
- Overture's Keyword Suggestion Tool (Yahoo!).
- Google Adwords Keyword Estimator.
- Google Insights for Search.
- Microsoft AdCenter Keyword Forcasting.

While these services will not be able to provide you with specific results when it comes to the amount of traffic each keyword will generate, they are able to provide you a clear-cut set of keywords to compare and contrast. Knowing that one word is more popular and has translated into higher results versus another option allows you to better determine which words you need to target in your search engine optimization.

Keyword difficulty

The second, and equally important, part of going through the process of keyword research is determining the keyword difficulty of the terms you are looking to utilise. Unfortunately, determining the difficulty of any keyword is a complicated process that has yet to be optimized for easy computation. When we talk about keyword difficulty, we are talking about how hard it will be to create a successful campaign for that specific word or phrase.

'Trying to pinpoint the exact popularity and resulting traffic from one specific keyword is an almost impossible task to achieve.'

In many cases, the more popular a keyword or phrase is will translate into the amount of difficulty one will have reaching the top rankings in search results for that keyword. This is simply because there are a number of other websites or organisations also trying to optimize the results on that one popular keyword.

Determining keyword difficulty, however, is not as simple as looking at the popularity because there are many larger and well-established sites that may not optimize for that specific keyword, but are still ranked high on the search engine indexes because of their large nature and existence on the Web. In many cases, website managers have found that it may be more profitable and beneficial to go after a number of different keywords with less difficulty, than trying to tackle a highly popular and more difficult keyword.

Choosing effective keywords

Choosing an effective set of keywords to target is the best way to ensure the success of your overall SEO campaign. By first determining a large set of keywords and phrases that are related to your website's content, you will be able to utilise research tools and create a smaller and more focused list of the most effective and easily optimized terms. It is important to look at all the factors, and to also remember that a number of less popular terms have the potential to reach more users than trying to utilise one or two very popular but much more difficult keywords.

What to avoid in keyword choices

There are a number of mistakes that are commonly made when choosing keywords to target for a website or page. It is important to be dynamic about the choices you make for the keywords and phrases that you are going to be targeting. While there are a number of keywords that may be searched very often and yield high results, it has been found that the majority of searches are the combination of less popular searches. These searches that are less common are called 'long tail' searches, and account for more than half of all searches.

Some of the most common mistakes that are made when selecting keywords and phrases to focus on include the following:

Targeting single-term words

Targeting single-term words or phrases is a mistake that many people make when trying to determine their keywords. Phrases that have two or three words provide you with a better chance of being ranked higher and also will direct more relevant traffic to your site. Compare it to how you search for something on the Internet; it is not common to use just one word to look for something specific, most successful searches are phrases or multiple terms.

Single words make it harder to be recognised for a couple of reasons. Firstly, they are too broad and, in many cases, can apply to a number of different circumstances or topics. The other problem with single-term keywords is that they are also very popular and it will be harder to find a way to outrank other websites also focused on these single-term keywords.

When looking at our example site, a number of keywords that would not yield great results because of their single-term nature would include:

- Workout.

'The second, and equally important, part of going through the process of keyword research is determining the keyword difficulty of the terms you are looking to utilise.'

- Fitness.

Instead it would be more effective to create multiple-term key phrases to focus on, such as:

- Women's fitness blog.
- Abdominal workout exercises.

Using overly broad terms

Another mistake that is made is choosing keywords or phrases that are too broad and do not apply enough to the content that your site contains. Terms that are too broad will display smaller results not only because they will have more competition, but because the user may be searching for a similar, but unrelated term. It is important to keep in mind the goal is not necessarily how many people see your site, but how many potential customers see your site – and there is a big difference.

Using terms that are too broad may very well bring a larger audience, but that audience will be less likely to be looking for your specific product or service. Instead it is important to use terms that are descriptive of your business or site. Adding the location of your business is a good way to minimise unwanted traffic, as well as other site-descriptive words.

Using overly specific terms

While you do not want your keywords and phrases to be too broad, you also want to be careful of making them too specific. It is important to get your targeted traffic to your site, but at the same time not exclude any potential traffic. It is clear that the number of people who search for a term is related to just how specific the term is. The connection can be made that with the more specific terms comes less popularity, meaning less people search for it as the competition goes down.

Terms that are too specific will find it less likely to be searched for. It is important to find a happy medium between specification and term-searching popularity.

'Choosing an effective set of keywords to target is the best way to ensure the success of your overall SEO campaign.'

Targeting terms that are not used often

It is important to take a look at how often terms are searched using tools such as the free Google Adwords program to look at the most searched terms. Choosing terms that are not searched for very often can end up being a waste of your time. Because these terms are not searched for, whatever effort you put in to targeting these terms will still not lead you to increased traffic.

Consider how many times the term is searched in comparison to other terms that can relate to your site. It is important to find terms that are searched, but are not overly popular and hard to make an impact with.

Targeting terms that are too popular

The opposite end of the spectrum is making the mistake of choosing to target words that are overly popular and have a lot of competition. We established that the more popular a word is, the more that word is used in a search and the more it turns into clicks and revenue. For websites that are starting out and trying to optimize their search results, choosing these words to target can be a big mistake.

If you choose search terms that are at the top of the list in ranking and popularity, it is likely that your site will be lost in the results. While these terms obviously yield a lot of searches, it is important to remember the 'long tail' searches, which amount to more than the most often searched terms. While these long tail terms are searched less often, when added into one group they vastly outnumber the popular terms. Utilising the information about long tail search terms is a great way to make an impact with your potential customers through search queries.

Summing Up

- Keyword research should be the first step in starting and crafting an SEO strategy or campaign, it is the foundation of a successful and well-laid plan.

- There are four main aspects of keyword research: realising your target audience, crafting keywords for that audience, analysing competition, and performing keyword queries.

- Keyword research is the process of investigating the keywords used by your target audience when utilising search engines.

- Keyword research is a vital part of learning about your target audience as well as how they think and navigate the Internet. It is an important part of developing a successful SEO strategy.

- When choosing which keywords to focus on, it is important to consider the keyword popularity. This can be related to the amount of traffic that is generated by searches for certain keywords.

- Keyword difficulty can be measured by how hard it would be to make an impact within a certain set of keywords. Difficulty increases with keyword popularity and frequent use by many different sites.

- There are a number of keyword research resources available to help determine current and past trends of keyword searches.

- Choosing an effective keyword is an important first step in creating a search engine optimization campaign that will be successful and have a large impact on search rankings.

- Do not choose keywords to target that are too broad or too specific as it will limit your results and website traffic.

- Remember that the 'long tail' keywords and phrases make up more of the overall search results than the more popular searches do.

- It is important to find a medium between popular phrases and 'long tail' phrases to target on your site.

Chapter Three

Design, Usability and Content

Design and development for search engine compatibility

While the technology behind search engines continues to develop and advance, there are still a number of limitations on how they are able to view and index the content on websites. It is these limitations that require website designers and developers to place a special emphasis on creating a website with content that is easily viewed and interpreted by search engines. The overall design, navigation and usability of a website has a large impact on just how the search engines view and interpret the website's value and how accurately it matches certain search terms.

There are a number of different ways that developers and website designers can create a site that is easily categorised and indexed by search engines. Optimizing the navigation, usability and overall design of a website can have a large impact on how frequently they are indexed by search engines which can translate to higher rankings within search queries. When striving for search engine optimization, the development, design and usability of a website is a vital aspect of maximising traffic received by matched search queries.

'The overall design, navigation and usability of a website has a large impact on just how the search engines view and interpret the website's value and how accurately it matches certain search terms.'

Easy-to-index content

As we previously discussed, every time a search query is entered into a search engine, the search engine searches through its indexes in order to locate the most accurate search results. In order for a website to be easily accessed it is necessary to have as much of your content as possible indexed within the search engine databases. While it is always important to have high-quality content, if that content is not easily indexed by search engine crawlers then it is more or less invisible to search queries.

When it comes to creating a site with content that is easy to index, it is important to keep in mind that HTML-created websites are the easiest to optimize and be recognised by search engines. Certain types of online content are more difficult for search engines to be able to index. Some of the types of online content that is not easily indexed include:

- Images and video.
- Flash files and sites.
- Java applets.
- Non-text content.

There are a number of ways that you can go about utilising these non-text forms of content and creating them in a way that can be more easily found and indexed by search engine crawlers. Images can be given 'alt attributes' using HTML which allow the description of the image to be visible to search engines. Content that is either auditory or visual can also be written in transcript form so the keywords and phrases can be accessed by both users and search engine crawlers.

Easy-to-crawl link structure

Search engines create their indexes by crawling, or spidering, online content by navigating through the link structures of websites. In order to fully optimize your website for search engine-generated traffic, it is important that your link structures allow for easy navigation for not only users, but also for web-crawling software used by search engines. Designing a website with an easy-to-crawl link structure provides you with the best chance of having your content seen, indexed and retrieved by search engines.

The importance of having an easy-to-crawl link structure is something that can have a large impact on both search engine results as well as website traffic. An easy-to-crawl link structure will provide both users and web crawlers with simple navigation and easy access to every part of the site. Creating text-based navigation, as well as anchor texting is a good basis for creating an easily navigated link structure.

The outcome of not optimizing the navigation and link structure of a site will result in pages that are left out, or not indexed by search engine web crawlers. It is important to make sure that all of the pages of the site have multiple internal and external links that are both linking to and from the page. In many cases having one link per page may stop search engines from finding the content important enough to index. This is why it is important to have multiple links for each visible page.

Common search engine compatibility issues

There are a number of common issues that websites run into when trying to design a search engine-compatible website. Since it is vital to have all pages easily accessed through a crawlable link structure, you must be aware of the common pitfalls to achieving easily indexed content. Some of the common issues website designers run into include the following:

▓ Links blocked by submission forms – Web-crawling software is unable to fill out and submit forms, which means any pages behind these forms will not be seen or indexed by search engines.

▓ Links viewable only by search – Web crawlers are unable to search for terms or pages, meaning links without additional ways to be seen will remain un-indexed.

▓ Flash and Java links – Links that are found within a Flash or Java site will remain unseen by search engine web crawlers and therefore not indexed.

'The outcome of not optimizing the navigation and link structure of a site will result in pages that are left out, or not indexed by search engine web crawlers.'

▨ Links on link-overloaded pages – Most web-crawling software will only go through the first 100 links found on a page. Link-overloaded pages will lessen the likelihood that your page is indexed by search engines.

Importance of usability and user experience

It is clear that the capabilities of search engines to grasp the entire feel and content of a website are limited, as they are only able to process certain website attributes. While the search engines look at factors such as placement of keywords and phrases, the site structure and the links found, it is important to keep in mind the overall user experience as well as the general usability of the site. By investigating the linking patterns of a particular website, search engines are able to create a number of different assumptions about the quality of that site.

'While the quality of a user's experience may not have a direct impact on how the search engine is able to access or index your site, they provide a strong outside influence on how search engines judge the site's value.'

While the quality of a user's experience may not have a direct impact on how the search engine is able to access or index your site, they provide a strong outside influence on how search engines judge the site's value. One of the clear benefits of creating a website with the user experience taken into consideration, is the site's popularity which also has an impact on how the search engines interpret quality. Designing a website which places the user experience as one of the top priorities will benefit in search engine rankings in a number of ways.

It is important to keep in mind that no matter how incredible the content is, if the website design and user experience is poor, no one will want to view or return to your site. There are so many sites with similar information that the choice of the user is often made by the design of the site, knowing that the information contained will be similar. Consider this, who would want to navigate a poorly designed site instead of one where information is easily and quickly accessed in a high-quality manner?

Another important benefit of having high-quality usability and user experience is how your website is shared with others. With social media taking an important role in Internet marketing, the quality of user experience has an even larger impact. Every time a link to your site is shared or posted on another website it provides search engines with yet another inbound link to your site from another. This will improve your ranking within search engines as it makes your site appear to indexes as of higher quality.

Catering content for SEO

One of the most common suggestions for achieving search engine optimization for a website is focusing on the creation of high-quality content. This has become such a common suggestion simply because it is one that has one of the largest impacts on how the sites are viewed, indexed and ranked by search engines. The goal of any search engine is to provide users with the most useful information for their specific search queries.

There are a number of reasons that Internet searches are performed, it is either to learn, understand, find, buy or solve. When search engines rank web pages within their results they strive to best answer the need of the user and place pages in the order that they think achieves this. Creating content that is catered to the needs of your user in a thorough way and with high quality, has a large impact on how search engines choose which sites to present to their users.

Catering content for your audience

Creating your content is another area that is greatly affected by the amount of research you do on your target audience. It is important to know how your audience operates, thinks, and the trends that are currently present within their demographics. When you create your content one of the most important aspects is that it appeals to the audience you are targeting. It is easy to make great content that is not applicable to your audience, however the results you receive will not likely be the ones that you desire.

Take in your target and marketed audience information while crafting your content. Think about the different ways your audience will search for, see and view your content. You want to be able to create content that your users will see as shareable. This means that it should be informative, in an interesting

'Creating content that is catered to the needs of your user in a thorough way and with high quality, has a large impact on how search engines choose which sites to present to their users.'

way that impacts their knowledge or thoughts on the topic. Bring a new and unique light upon subjects that have been previously talked about by linking them to other related topics.

Using our example website www.tonyasfitnessonline.com, here is an example to help compare audience-crafted content. As we stated previously, our target audience is women aged 18-35, working, stay-at-home and college-aged.

Content without our audience in mind:

- Exercise articles about building larger muscles through lifting weights – While it does hit on exercise, and muscle building, our audience of women is most likely more focused on toning and losing weight than building muscles.

Content with our audience in mind:

- Easy at-home exercises that can tone your waist and oblique – Women aged 18-35 are focused on toning the abdominal area and love handles, this would better suit our particular target audience.

- News article reports that exercising briefly in the morning increases energy and metabolism throughout the day – This is a topic that would interest women in our audience, and also provides an opportunity to link out of the site to another trusted fitness site.

Summing Up

- The overall design and basic development of your web page will directly relate to how well search engines are able to view and index your site's content.

- Your site design should keep in mind two vital aspects in order to optimize your SEO: an easy-to-crawl link structure and content that is easily indexed.

- HTML-based websites are the easiest for search engines to navigate and index. When using more complex methods of web design there are additional steps needed in order to make content easily indexable.

- The user experience and overall usability of the site will have an indirect effect on the success of the website search rankings through sharing and recommending of your site by users.

- One of the most important suggestions to follow within SEO is to create content that is catered for search engine optimization. This means creating high-quality content that is directly relatable to your keywords and phrases.

Chapter Four

Link Popularity and Page Rankings

What is link popularity?

When it comes to SEO, one of the most important factors to include in your strategy is that of link popularity and page rankings. In the eyes of search engines, links serve as the connectors between the pages and sites. Search engines utilise link analysis in order to find out what pages are linked or related to each other and how those pages are related to each other.

In addition, the amount of links that connect to a certain page are in a way considered as 'votes' made by Internet users who choose to view those sites. It is these 'votes' that are used by search engines to help determine the popularity of a site or specific page. As technology has improved and advanced, the methods for link data analysis have become more intricate and include various and complex algorithms. It is these algorithms that serve as the evaluations of web pages and sites based on the data they collect.

What elements of a link do search engines consider?

While it is difficult to fully understand all of the different factors and aspects that a search engine considers when weighing the importance of links, research enables us to make certain assumptions about the measurements. There are a

'Search engines utilise link analysis in order to find out what pages are linked or related to each other and how those pages are related to each other.'

number of factors that are commonly considered to be ranked high on the list of importance when determining the quality of links. Some of these factors include the following:

- Website popularity is one main factor that is put into the equation of determining link validity. The more popular, visited and important a site is, the more importance the links stemming from that site will have for search engines.

- Content specific popularity is another aspect that is considered when weighing the importance of an inbound link. What this means is that a link stemming from a site that carries a lot of weight within a certain topic or specific content will matter more than a more popular site that does not match the link's content.

- Trusted sites will impact your inbound link popularity more than sites with little or no history and reputation. A link from a site that is trusted and known not to be spam will have a much larger impact.

- Anchor text is one of the largest factors that search engines look at when ranking the strength of a link signal. When many sites link to a certain page with corresponding keywords, the result will be a higher ranking for that set of words.

Link quality over quantity

It is important to understand that link popularity is not only measured by the amount of links that are created to and from your page or site, but is also impacted by the quality of those links. There are two different ways that the quality of the inbound links makes a difference on how they affect the search engine optimization of your site.

The first quality measure considered when looking at link popularity is focused on the context of the link that is connected to your site. In order to improve your ranking in relation to certain search terms, it is important to get inbound links from sites and pages that relate to the terms you are focusing on. Inbound links that come from pages or sites that have little or no relation to the topic your site is promoting will have a very minimal effect on your page's ranking with the designated keywords and phrases.

'It is important to understand that link popularity is not only measured by the amount of links that are created to and from your page or site, but is also impacted by the quality of those links.'

The second quality measure to keep in mind is the ranking of the pages and sites your inbound links are coming from. By simple association it is easy to see that lower ranking sites would likely be linked to other lower ranking sights. With this in mind, think about how much larger the impact would be if your site was linked to a high-ranking page or site. It is much more beneficial for your search ranking and quality of traffic to have links coming in from other high-ranking sights with relatable content.

What's the importance of link popularity?

While the factors that search engines have considered in the past when evaluating websites and pages was more focused on on-page information, as technology advances there is more emphasis being placed on external, or off-page, factors. One of the main off-page factors that is looked at and considered when creating search results is that of link popularity. Many search engines such as Google utilise the amounts of links to and from a page as well as the type of link when creating the ranking of search results.

The increase of emphasis on off-page attributes when calculating page and website quality has made growing your site's link popularity a critical part of a successful search engine optimization campaign. Increasing link popularity through link building is one of the best ways to gain increased visibility, traffic and attention from search engines. Link popularity has become one of the top priorities of improving your site's traffic as well as search ranking.

'One of the main off-page factors that is looked at and considered when creating search results is that of link popularity.'

How do you build link popularity?

Now that we have established the importance of building link popularity and the impact it can have on your page's search rankings, the question becomes – how do you effectively execute this task? There are a number of different ways that one can go about creating more link building in order to increase link popularity. While some of them are as easy as submitting website information to search engines and other platforms, others take more time and additional effort.

One of the first steps to building your link popularity is by locating websites that relate to your page in one way or another. Focus on a number of keywords or phrases you are going after and find sites that are both ranked high in search results but also have good supporting content that would relate to users interested in your site's information. Sites like these could include newsgroups or group forums that talk about pertinent topics or issues relating to your page.

Adding content with a signature featuring your page's or site's URL is an easy way to get additional traffic, and also to be further indexed by web crawlers. The more you post within the forum the more your page will gain incoming links and page impressions. Another way to gain more inbound links is through writing and publishing articles for websites that discuss similar issues or topics. In most cases you are allowed to include a URL at the end of your article, which will also help to build links.

'Adding content with a signature featuring your page's or site's URL is an easy way to get additional traffic, and also to be further indexed by web crawlers.'

Link popularity with Google and PageRank

Google is currently the most popular search engine on the Internet and has also been an industry leader in terms of search result rankings, especially when it comes to using link popularity as a factor. While almost all of the major search engines utilise some form of link popularity to determine search rankings, Google puts a higher amount of emphasis on the importance of link popularity when ranking websites.

In terms of Google, PageRank indicates the overall link popularity of a site. It is a way for Google to measure the quality of a site and then rank it accordingly within a set of search results. This method of link analysis is only available to Google as it was patented by Stanford University who sold the rights to Google. The overall PageRank of a website is based on the combined PageRank of each individual page within the site, as they are seen as separate entities when being looked at in terms of link popularity.

How to use Google as a resource

Google provides users with a number of tools and resources when it comes to measuring the link popularity of a site. The Google Toolbar is a plugin available for Internet Explorer that allows users to see a number of different factors and measurements of the URL that a user is currently on, including the page rank and inbound links.

Summing Up

- Link popularity is one of the methods which search engines utilise in order to determine the value of a website by looking at the inbound and outbound links to a site and a page.

- When it comes to link popularity, each page is viewed as a separate entity, therefore both internal site links as well as external links are viewed and considered when determining the page's value.

- There are a number of different factors considered by search engines when formulating the value of links both on-page and off-page. Some of these factors include overall website popularity and ranking, content specific popularity, how trusted the sites are, as well as the anchor text behind the links.

- Link popularity is an important part of SEO as the majority of search engines utilise it in order to determine the value of pages and the search ranking for specific keyword searches.

- Google was the pioneer of using link popularity as a measurable quality within web pages and offers a number of resources for measuring and improving websites' link popularity, including their PageRank programs.

- While part of link popularity is judged by the amount of links both linking into and out of your site, it is important to consider the quality of the link over the sheer number of links. A trusted and valued link into your site will mean more than a dozen less valuable links.

Chapter Five

Link Building

What is the importance of link building?

In the last chapter we determined that link popularity is an important way to establish more credibility within search engine rankings. Now the challenge becomes how to successfully build your website's incoming link structure, also known as backlink profile, to optimize this aspect in terms of SEO. Link building is a part of SEO that can be difficult and challenging to properly execute, but at the same time is one of the most important. High-quality link building can help your website achieve success that lasts over time.

Link building is one of the most effective ways of increasing your link popularity and overall search ranking. Through the creation of a backlink profile that is vast and extensive, you are able to produce the best possible search engine results. There are many different methods to achieving the best possible link building for your site and it is important to understand which method will work best for your specific situation.

External link building

Understanding the different methods of link building is the first step to determining which ones will work the best for your website. There are three basic types of link building that can be used to enhance your website's backlink profile.

The three basic types of external link building are:

- ▧ Self-created.
- ▧ Suggested and approved.

'Link building is a part of SEO that can be difficult and challenging to properly execute, but at the same time is one of the most important. High-quality link building can help your website achieve success that lasts over time.'

▨ Editorial.

Self-created link building

Self-created link building includes any type of link or posting with a link that is put out there by a website manager or SEO professional. There are thousands of different websites and online communities that allow for posting a web address. The links may be posted within a user profile, online forums, visitor books, or even comments made on a blog. This would also include the creation of articles written and published on blogs which contain links or website URLs.

Suggested and approved link building

Suggested and approved link building refers to any type of site, program or directory that allows the submission of URLS whether it be paid or unpaid. This can be done in a number of ways, while there are websites in which URLs need to be submitted to become a part of, other ways include emailing bloggers or other writers manually in order to get a link posted on the site or within an article.

Editorial link building

Editorial link building refers to the links that are manifested through content or company references without any prompting or request made on your behalf. This type of link building cannot be directly impacted by your website staff, but rather is the outcome of creating material and content that is worthy of being referenced in other places.

How to start a link building campaign

With any type of Internet marketing campaign, it is important to create a set of goals and strategies when beginning. The same assumption applies to a link building campaign, however it is made more difficult by the fact that link building is one of the hardest aspects of a search engine optimization campaign to measure. For many of those new to the industry, it is going to take a little bit of trial and error to find out what will be the best method for your specific campaign. However, there are a number of metrics that are available to be used in order to maximise the return on time, energy and money spent on creating a strong backlink profile.

Having a clear set of goals, as well as a proposed timeline of when these goals should be achieved, is a good start to establishing the beginning of a link building campaign. This should be accompanied by a number of strategies focused on the execution of these goals.

Link building methods

There are a number of different strategies that can be used when creating a strong backlink profile. While some are more effective than others in different situations, all have a potential to increase your page ranking as well as your site's overall visibility. When beginning a campaign, it is a good idea to utilise many different types of link building methods and determine through trial and error which is going to be most effective for your site as well as your long-term goals.

Discussion forums and blogs commentary

Blogs and discussion forums have become a large part of the online community and can be found in almost any topic or industry. By doing a little research you will be able to locate popular blogs and forums, which relate to your site. By becoming an active member and commentator within these blogs and forums you will likely be able to place signatures to your posts which include a direct link to your site. Remember that while a link to your site's home page is always beneficial, search engines see each page on your site as an individual, so try varying which URLs you include.

'Having a clear set of goals, as well as a proposed timeline of when these goals should be achieved is a good start to establishing the beginning of a link building campaign.'

Writing articles and press releases

The creation of external content is one that has become a popular method of creating more buzz and search engine attention for your website and organisation. There are a number of different benefits that can be seen through the creation of articles and press releases. While some sites will opt to publish these within their site as well as on linked external sites, others will work towards having articles and press releases published on sites that are otherwise unrelated to their business.

There are a number of services available to assist in the expanded publication of press releases so that the content will be able to reach a more topic-concentrated group as well as a larger group of Internet users. External content that is of high-quality also allows for the opportunity to be referenced or used as a source by other authors and websites covering similar topics.

'The creation of external content is one that has become a popular method of creating more buzz and search engine attention for your website and organisation.'

Social media and viral marketing

Social media has become one of the most popular aspects of Internet use and it is important to be able to properly utilise all that this has to offer. Social media not only provides you with free or very inexpensive advertising, but it also gives you the opportunity to know your target audience. By doing a little research you will be able to determine the most appropriate way to share your site as well as increase your backlink profile through social media outlets such as Twitter, Facebook and Pinterest.

Each time your content is shared you will have added a link incoming into your site that is available to be crawled and indexed by search engines. If you combine your other link building methods with this form of online advertising you are able to better maximise the outcome of this aspect of SEO.

Directory submissions

Directory submissions are the most straight forward way to create a link building profile, and will be the most effective for sites that are smaller and have less competition. There are a number of directories that allow your site to be included for free or for a nominal cost. While any link incoming to your site is valued, it is important to weigh the cost with the benefits.

What external link building method is best for my site?

Different methods of link building are more effective for certain types of websites, while they may be less effective for others. The type of methods that you choose to implement depends on a couple of different factors including the nature of your website as well as the scale of the site. The methods that will be effective for smaller websites are, in many cases, ineffective for sites that are larger and have more competition.

Smaller websites will benefit from almost any type of link building methods. Manual link building such as submissions into directories, asking sites to add links as well as link exchanges could all have an impact on the search rankings for that site. However, when it comes to sites that are larger and more complex, there is going to need to be a different approach. Larger sites require larger solutions, which may include extensive sets of articles, or the creation of high-quality blogs and community forums.

What are internal links?

An internal link is any hyperlink that connects, or points, to another page within the same website domain. An example of this would be the home page containing a link that connected to the 'About Us' page. When using internal links it is good practice to be careful of the anchor text that is used to link to the page. Search engines look at and rank pages according to the content inside, including the anchor text.

Anchor text

When creating internal links, an important factor to remember is to use anchor text to describe what the link is connecting to. The anchor text is the text that represents a hyperlink but is visible to the user. Anchor text is usually written in blue and underlined to indicate that it is a link. When within source code anchor text appears the following way:

<a href=http://www.TonyasFitnessOnline.com">Tonya's Fitness </a>

Anchor text is an important aspect of SEO, as search engines really rely on the text for both internal and external links in order to rank the pages in search engine results. Optimizing your anchor text along with your internal link building is a good formula for creating a website with material and content that is easily found by users as well as indexed by search engine crawlers and bots.

'When creating internal links, an important factor to remember is to use anchor text to describe what the link is connecting to. The anchor text is the text that represents a hyper link but is visible to the user.'

Why is internal link building important?

Internal link building is an essential part of creating a website that is easy to be crawled through by search engines and then recorded in their keyword-based indexes. Your internal links are what will guide these crawlers to your important information and also give them a sense of the content within your site. Building links to create a stronger site architecture is the best way to create a site where search engines can easily access all of your pages and information.

Link building does not only help with your site's navigation and usability, but also has the chance to impact your overall search ability and ranking. Search engines look at all links, both internal and external, that are pointing at a specific page. Having a number of internal links pointing at the specific pages within your own domain will help with the search engine's ranking of that page as well as your overall site. Pairing internal link building with high-quality anchor text is a great way to improve your rankings in search results for your targeted keywords and topics.

What is the best way to build links internally?

Internal links are the best way to create a site architecture that is compatible with SEO. Building links internally should be done in a way that will be easy to be crawled and referenced by search engines as well as users. It is important to create a link plan that is easily followed. Many people believe the ideal structure would be that of a pyramid structure because of a couple of reasons. The pyramid structure as shown below not only provides an easy road map, but limits the links to the homepage. This will help create more ranking power for the other pages.

Example website: www.tonyasfitnessonline.com

START DIAGRAM

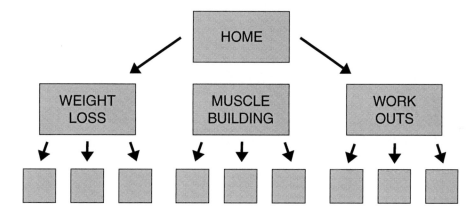

'Internal links are the best way to create a site architecture that is compatible with SEO.'

END DIAGRAM

Combining the use of both high-quality link structure as well as a good usage of keywords and phrases in anchor text will help provide the highest results. When linking to pages on a certain topic, the anchor text on the link should properly describe where you are linking. This is important for both user experience as well as the ability of search engines to properly index the material and provide high-quality answers within their results.

Using the Tonya's Fitness Online website as an example it would appear as this:

Internal link: www.tonyasfitnessonline.com/workouts/flatabdominalexercises

Anchor text: Get flat abs.

Summing Up

- Because there is such an emphasis placed on the value of link popularity when determining the page rankings and search rankings for websites, it is necessary to optimize on this factor through the process of link building.

- Link building includes a number of different methods to increase the amount of inbound links to your website or pages in order to develop a strong backlink profile.

- There are three main categories when it comes to link building: self-created, suggested and approved, and editorial link building.

- When starting a link building campaign it is important to set up a goal structure and timeline as well as strategies on how to best achieve improvement for your specific site type and size.

- Some of the most common link building methods include starting a blog, writing articles on topic-relevant material, viral or social media marketing, directory submission, forum submissions and press releases.

- Larger websites will require a more extensive link building strategy, while smaller or start-up websites will benefit from almost any type of link building method.

- Internal links are a vital part of creating a website that is fully optimized for SEO purposes.

- Internal links can be used to improve site architecture as well as create a site navigation that is easy to follow for both users as well as search engine crawlers.

- Internal links should be paired with well-written and planned anchor text.

- Anchor text is often used by search engines to better determine the content within a page as well as the content the link is pointing to.

- Internal links that are created with the pyramid shape in mind will have the best chance of gaining higher rankings as well as being indexed by search engines more often.

Chapter Six

On-Page Search Engine Optimization

What is on-page SEO?

While aspects such as link building are important off-page factors considered by search engines, there are a number of different on-page factors that also have a large impact on the effectiveness of an SEO campaign. On-page SEO refers to anything that is actually within the website or web pages that is utilised to improve the site's search rankings and overall popularity. On-page SEO includes a variety of methods that will help to create a site that is best viewed and ranked by search engines.

It is important to remember that both on-page and off-page search engine optimization methods are necessary to truly improve your search ranking and create a high-quality and easy-to-find website. One type of optimization without the other will yield much smaller results and will be overall less effective. Throughout this chapter we will look at the variety of techniques that can be used to optimize your on-page SEO.

'On-page SEO refers to anything that is actually within the website or web pages that is utilised to improve the site's search rankings and overall popularity.'

How does your page copy affect on-page SEO?

Everything that is written on your website is recorded by search engines. This means that all of your copy is recorded and searched for keywords and key phrases in order to be properly indexed by search engines. Since the goal of a search engine is to provide their users with the most relevant information, the actual text that you have on your pages is vital to ranking higher in search engine results.

Creating a site that has interesting and captivating content is one of the largest factors that can influence the amount of activity your site sees within search results. Good and high-quality content are not items that can be ignored during the SEO process. Users can easily tell the difference between good content and poorly crafted content, and in a way the quality of your content is advertising in itself. Good content is more likely to be shared with others, and will help your users better understand the topic, and maybe even want to learn more about it.

When writing content it is important to not only stick to one set of keywords and phrases, but consider the user and how they would search for and relate to the content differently. It is important to use a variety of keywords and phrases that relate to your content. For example, the use of synonyms is a good way to create new keyword variations that may be used within the search terms.

When creating content keep in mind the following tips:

- Use unique and easy-to-read content – Content that is too complex, or is poorly written and has many errors will inhibit the user from wanting to read more, or being able to understand. Create content that is high in quality and completely unique, it will give the user a better reason to return to your site looking for more information.

- Craft content around your users, not search engines – While you want to be found by search engines, they are not the ones actually reading your content for information and knowledge, your users are. Create your content with the user in mind, don't overuse keywords just to get them on the page, create an understandable and identifiable piece of writing that will help you connect with your users.

What are heading tags and how are they helpful?

Heading tags are a part of HTML that can be used as a way to highlight important words or sentences. They are not the same as the <head> tag and are separate from HTML headers. You can use heading tags in different sizes that are represented by <h1> through to <h6>. The effect of heading tags is to highlight information, and commonly to change the size of the font accordingly.

Heading tags are a great way to help guide the user to the information that is most important and in what order they should visually look at the page. Keep in mind that when you are using heading tags to not overuse them. Too many heading tags may make it harder for the user instead of easier.

What are title tags?

Title tags are used in HTML website creation as a way to let users as well as search engines know what the subject of a particular page is. Each page of your website should have its own individual title tag to describe that page. When writing HTML the <title> tag can be found within the <head> tag. Below is an example of how a title tag would look inside the HTML of the home page for our example site.

```
<html>

<head>

<title>Tonya's Fitness – Find Exercises, Workouts and Fitness Advice
</>title>

<meta name=...>

</head>

<body>
```

In this example, the title of our home page will appear to be exactly what is written within the <title> tag. This home page title is usually the first line of text that appears within search engine results so it is important to create a title tag that has the most important and relevant information.

'Keep in mind that when you are using heading tags to not overuse them. Too many heading tags may make it harder for the user instead of easier.'

How do title tags affect on-page SEO?

There are a number of different aspects of a web page that are considered by search engines when ranking the results of a query; one of the most important of these is the title tag. The title tag is that short description that accompanies the website name and is usually seen above the URL of the website. This is one of the most important and influential aspects considered by search engines when ranking websites. The title of your web pages is the first thing that users will see when using a search engine, it is usually the first line of a result and is underlined and written in blue.

The words found in the title tag are the first to be looked at and indexed by search engines. When you utilise a set of keywords within a title tag, search engines will bold these words in the search results of any query that matches those words. This will translate to higher visibility for the site as well as increase the likelihood of receiving a click from the search user.

It has been found that using keywords within your title tag is the first and most important step in getting noticed by search engines. Creating a high-quality and descriptive title tag full of specific keywords will allow engines to easily recognise and index your content, making the visibility better as well as increasing search rankings for those words or phrases.

'It has been found that using keywords within your title tag is the first and most important step in getting noticed by search engines.'

How to optimize your title tags

Because title tags play such a large role in the search engine's ranking methods, it is important to place an emphasis on how to best optimize these for search engine consumption. There are a number of different methods to use when creating a title tag that will serve as an effective description of your site.

Straight to the point – When creating title tags, one of the most important aspects is creating a unique tag that relays all of the information. Make sure that you describe what is on the page accurately and use descriptive words. A title tag should be short and sweet, but get across the content and site attributes.

Length of your title tag – While the maximum amount of characters that will be displayed within the search results is 70, some sites opt to include additional characters. This may be useful for sites that are trying to include additional keywords or phrases within their title tag, but will remain unviewed within search results by Internet users. It is recommended that you stay within the 70-character limit when creating a title tag unless you need to include certain keywords to impact your search ranking in those areas.

Location of keywords – Where the most important keywords are within your title tag will have an impact on your search ranking as well as your user experience. This will hold especially true if you are going over the 70-character limit. Because users will only see the first 70 characters it is important to place the most emphasised keywords towards the front of your title tag. This will increase the likelihood that a user will click on your link for that specific information and will help with important keyword rankings.

Include a unique brand name – Title tags are a great place to include your specific company or brand name. This will help to make your brand name more visible and will also push clicks from users who already know this name and trust it. Even if your brand has yet to be established, this is a good way to get the name out there, especially when it is paired with other important keywords.

Readability – While it is great to include all of your important keywords within your title tag, you need to pay attention to how the tag reads to search engine users. It is the first glimpse users will get into your website and can easily be the reason that they decide to click on your link instead of a link to a different and similar site. Consider the impact of a first impression when creating a title tag and format it in a manner that is intriguing and informative.

What are meta tags?

Meta tags are another way to further describe what the contents of the web page are in a brief summary. It usually appears below the title of the page in search results as a further description of the page's contents. It can be

'Where the most important keywords are within your title tag will have an impact on your search ranking as well as your user experience.'

anywhere between a couple of sentences to a short paragraph. Within HTML the <meta> tag can be found beneath the <title> tag and within the <head> tag as shown on the next page.

```
<html>

<head>

<title>Tony's Fintess - Find Exercises, Workouts and Fitness Advice
</>title>

<meta name= "description=" content ="Tonya's Fitness has at-home
exercise videos, daily workouts, fitness articles and monthly weight loss
goals. We also have an online fitness community and free member forums.
">

</head>

<body>
```

The meta tag is a great way to get users interested and intrigued enough to click on your link and view your site. Describe what is on that specific page in a readable way. Avoid filling your meta tags with only keywords, or content that is not directly related to the actual written copy on that particular page. Assign a meta tag for each individual page of your website.

How do meta tags affect on-page SEO?

In the past meta tags had a lot more emphasis placed on them than they do today in the world of SEO. When search engine rankings were first established along with the Internet, they were one of the main factors considered by search engines when creating a search results page. However, since the technology has developed, less emphasis has been placed on these types of tags and they are considered to have a much smaller impact on the actual search engine page results ranking. With that being said it is still worth looking at the different kinds of meta tags when it comes to on-page SEO.

The two main types of meta tags to consider are:

- Meta description.
- Meta keywords.

The meta description tag can be described as a short synopsis of the content of that specific page. While search engines no longer use these tags as a method of determining the rank of your page, they are most commonly used as the small blurb that is displayed directly below a link on the search result page. When creating these tags consider that they are really advertising copy that can be used to lure users in to clicking on your link and visiting your site. With this in mind you should create your meta tags as a readable and intriguing piece of text.

Meta keywords are the less important of the two main types of meta tags, and had a lot more value at the beginning of search engine use. They were previously used as the way to present search engines with a list of keywords that represent the site. However, over the years the technology of search engines have placed little or no emphasis on this aspect and instead are using much more insightful technology which we have and will continue to discuss. However, they are simple to create and will not harm your website's ranking.

What are image tags?

Using images and video on your website is a great way to create more interest and an overall more user-friendly site. It is important to realise that you can easily use these images to help with SEO. Image tags are the tags used within HTML to describe the image that is seen on the page by users. The filename of the image is automatically in the HTML when the image is added, and an image tag allows you to further describe what the image or video shows. The example below shows how the source code would appear with and without the added 'alt' attribute.

- Without the 'alt' attribute:

<img src= "pushup.gif">

- With the 'alt' attribute:

<img src= "pushup.gif" alt= "Proper Pushup Position"/>

With the 'alt' attribute, search engines will be able to index the photos for your site by the keywords you use to describe them.

How do image tags help on-page optimization?

Image tags give you another way of getting noticed by search engines for the content on your site. In order to optimize your website's images you can utilise the 'alt' attribute. What this does is allow your image to have a separate description from the actual file name of the image. Search engines can use the 'alt' attribute assigned to your image as a way to further index your site to apply to certain searches. It also helps your images to be recognised by image search results such as Google Images.

URL structure

URLs are the specific web address for a page within your site and can have a large impact on search ability and page ranking. It is important to create a URL with SEO in mind as it is the first thing that search engines will see. There are a number of different ways that you can maximize the effect that your URL has on search engine crawlers. The easiest and most important is by utilising your main keywords within your URLs.

Let's take a look at our sample website for 'Tonya's Fitness'. We want to create a URL that contains our company name as well as keywords in a simple way.

- The URL www.TonyasFitnessOnline.com allows us to include the name, the area of focus (fitness) as well as the fact it is an online fitness resource.

The initial URL is the first link that users and search engines are likely to see, however when search engines crawl the Internet they also look at all of the pages as individuals. That is why it is also important to consider how the URLs appear for each of the pages within your website. Make sure to assign a specific and descriptive page name to each page. When looking at our example site we can see the differences between an SEO-effective URL and one that inhibits SEO.

'URLs are the specific web address for a page within your site and can have a large impact on search ability and page ranking. It is important to create a URL with SEO in mind as it is the first thing that search engines will see.'

- The URL: www.TonyasFitnessOnline.com/page/9277438fyl3392 – While it still has the main URL with keywords and company name, it does not provide any description of the actual page, just the numerical web address. This would make it hard for search engines to index that page.

- The URL: www.TonyasFitnessOnline.com/workoutvideos/TricepsandBiceps –

This is a search engine-optimized URL structure. It not only provides the fact that the page contains workout videos, but also includes the keywords 'triceps' and 'biceps'. This will make indexing by search engines easy and return more search results.

When creating a URL structure, remember to always use descriptive words instead of page numbers. It gives users a better idea of what they are clicking on, and if it is actually what they are looking for. It also gives search engines a better chance of properly indexing the site and its content.

Summing Up

- A combination of high-quality on-page and off-page optimization is required to create a multidimensional and successful SEO campaign

- On-page optimization consists of three main aspects, title tags, meta tags and URL structure.

- Title tags are one of the most important parts of on-page optimization. Creating a well-written and keyword-dense title tag will help your website appear high on the search result rankings.

- Meta tags are being used less by search engines to determine rankings, but still hold importance in providing a descriptive piece for users on the content within your web page or site.

- Utilising keywords within your URL structure will help search engines better locate and index your page and the content within it appropriately and in the right categories.

Chapter Seven

Search Engine Tools

Importance of using available search engine tools

Search engines want to be able to easily crawl and index websites so that they can continually provide the highest amount of service to their users. In order to best achieve this, every major search engine has provided webmasters with a number of tools to help in the research and measurement of how to best create sites that will rank high on the search results page. They have established a number of different support and guidance tools that are readily made available for anyone to take advantage of.

While some of these tools may provide more of a benefit for certain sites than others, it is a good idea to get a general grasp of what each tool could do for you and your site. Because these sites are created and developed by the specific search engine, they are able to provide insight that otherwise would be unachievable. It is important to use these tools in order to create the best SEO which will have the largest impact.

'Sitemaps are a great way to point search engines in the right direction when it comes to properly crawling through your website for indexable content and pages.'

Search engine sitemaps

Sitemaps are a great way to point search engines in the right direction when it comes to properly crawling through your website for indexable content and pages. It is basically like creating a roadmap for how you want search engines to see the content you have made available and to easily access it.

There are three main types of sitemaps:

- XML sitemaps.

- RSS sitemaps.
- Txt sitemaps.

XML sitemaps are the most recommended type of sitemap to utilise and are made up of extensible mark-up language. The benefits to creating this type of site map include that it is the preferred and most accepted type of format for sitemaps. It makes the search engine's job of crawling through the site easy, and can be reproduced for many different search engine models. The main negative for this type of sitemap is that it requires a large file size.

RSS site maps, also known as really simple syndication, are another type of accepted format. These are much easier to create and to keep track of as they can be set to update automatically whenever a website is updated or new content is put into place. Some users find that this format is more difficult to manage compared to XML sitemaps.

Txt sitemaps are the most simple form of sitemaps and are simply a text file. They are easy to understand and manage, as each URL is one separate line and can hold as many as 50,000 lines. However the drawback of this is that you are unable to add meta data to these files.

Google Webmaster tools

Google has set the bar for other search engines when it comes to providing their users with a number of different tools needed to optimize their Web impact. Google provides users with tools to research their target demographic through geographic locations as well as statistics on the following aspects of SEO:

- Web crawl.
- Mobile crawl.
- Content analysis.
- Link data.
- Statistics.

Web crawl is a diagnostic tool that can be used to see where Google had issues when trying to crawl through a specific site. It is a great way to check your site structure and link structure in order to perform better in search rankings. A similar tool is their Mobile Crawl which will provide the same information for mobile compatible sites.

Google's content analysis is a great way to help sites identify whether or not they have any components within their site that prohibit search engines from accessing all the content. This includes any HTML that is not search engine-friendly as well as issues with title tags and descriptions.

Yahoo! Site Explorer

Yahoo!'s Site Explorer offers significantly less information when it comes to analytics and diagnostics of a website. However, they do provide you with a number of statistics about your site including the title tag impact as well as the number of pages on your site that are actually being crawled and indexed within their databases. They also provide you with the option to add your URL or feed directly to Yahoo! which is a great benefit for sites that utilise blogs and frequently update content and information.

Bing Webmaster tools

Bing Webmaster Center provides you with a number of different tools to help optimize your search results and gauge the effectiveness of your website. They provide users with a method of creating a profile for their sitemaps as well as additional information such as contact numbers if there are problems when Bing attempts to crawl and index their sites.

Bing also provides a lot of help when it comes to identifying and fixing any crawl issues that arise. This includes pointing out obvious HTTP status errors, any type of meta robots.txt efforts as well as identifying unsupported content and any type of malware issues found on pages or sites.

Similar to Yahoo! and Google, Bing offers the chance to submit sitemaps to their database but also provides tools to help discover what keywords are being linked to their specific sites through search queries and results. There

'Google's content analysis is a great way to help sites identify whether or not they have any components within their site that prohibit search engines from accessing all the content.'

are also tools available through Bing that will help create a better backlink profile and to locate and identify both incoming and outgoing links to their website and individual web pages.

Summing Up

- It is important to take advantage of the tools that are offered through online search engines as they are a good insight into potential problems and areas for improvement.

- Creating sitemaps is the easiest way to correctly point search engines in the right direction and help them to crawl through and index all of your site's content.

- There are three types of sitemaps: XML, RSS and Txt. XML is the most accepted and thorough of these three types.

- Google, Yahoo! and Bing all offer unique and important analytic and diagnostic tools that can have a large impact on realising important areas of needed improvement as well as potential problems and issues.

Chapter Eight

Tracking and Measuring SEO

Importance of tracking and measuring your campaign

When it comes to any type of marketing campaign, one of the most important parts is the measuring and tracking of the campaign's success. Without measuring the effectiveness of a campaign, you will have no way of knowing which aspects have been successful and should be repeated versus which ones have little to no impact on the outcome. It is important that by measuring the success of a campaign you are able to better improve those areas which are lacking and create an even stronger Web presence.

The tracking and measuring of your SEO campaign should be included in your overall goal and strategy timeline that you created at the beginning. It will enable you to compare and contrast the strategies you utilised and whether or not they met the goals that you had set out beforehand. There are a number of different methods that SEO professionals use in order to track and measure the success and effectiveness.

'Without measuring the effectiveness of a campaign, you will have no way of knowing which aspects have been successful and should be repeated versus which ones have little to no impact on the outcome.'

Type of measurements to track for SEO

While every website and organisation is a little bit different, there are a number of measurements that will apply to almost any type of site when it comes to search engine optimization. It is important to look at these measurements and determine what has been effective and what needs to still be improved further.

Source of incoming site traffic

There are three main types of source traffic that will come into your website and it is important to keep a record every month of how your traffic is spread out between these three areas:

- Search engine traffic, originating from a search query.

- Referral traffic, originating from other sites, emails or promotional links.

- Direct navigation, originating from typed-in URLs and bookmarks.

Keeping track of this information will help you to determine which areas your website is struggling with, as well as give you a source of comparison over a set period of time. It is a good way to see the general trend of traffic to your site as well as a way to measure marketing efforts.

'It is important to measure the amount of traffic you receive from each of the major search engines.'

Specific search engine visits

It is important to measure the amount of traffic you receive from each of the major search engines for a number of reasons. This will allow you to access additional insight about your audience and which search engine provides the most amount of traffic from their queries to your site. Being able to see the specific impact each engine has on your traffic and search rankings will help you to discover and fix any potential issues you are having with your SEO.

Because each search engine uses a slightly different approach to evaluating websites' search page ranking, looking into each specific search engine results will help to discover which methods worked the best on each site. For example, Google focuses more on off-page optimization such as link analysis, whereas Yahoo! and Bing often rely more heavily on on-page optimization and site structure. It is important to realise that this information can help you to discover which areas you need to improve upon in order to get the best SEO for each search engine.

Measuring specific keywords and terms

One of the most important parts to measure within an SEO campaign is the effectiveness of the keywords and phrases that you focus on and utilise. Keeping track of the visits that are generated because of searches for certain keywords will help you to develop a set of terms that is most beneficial to your website traffic.

It is important to measure the visits generated by these terms and phrases on a regular basis, and more often than other measurements. This is a way to continually perform keyword research that will have a large impact on your key audience and SEO. Tracking this information is a way to get into the heads of your target audience as well as determine just how well you have targeted the necessary keywords to help build traffic and reputation.

Specific search terms and conversion rates

Another aspect to keep in mind when creating measurable and traceable efforts within SEO is that of the link between specific search terms and the conversion rates they create. When we talk about conversion rates we are discussing the difference between the amount of searches that include your page compared to the amount of clicks to your site those search queries produce. In many instances certain search terms or phrases will lead to higher conversion rates than others.

While some search terms may put you at the top of the search results page, they may not provide a high conversion rate for one reason or another. It is important to connect the amount of clicks as well as the overall ranking in search results when looking at your specific keywords and phrases that you are working on targeting. This will provide you with the knowledge necessary to improve your actual revenue, or reach goals of traffic and site visitors.

Summing Up

- Without putting specific measurements and tracking in place, you will be unable to see if the SEO campaign has been effective and garnered the results you need.

- It is a good idea to set up your desired goals in these measurements before the beginning of your campaign so you are able to compare your actions to your results.

- Directly compare each goal to the strategy and method you used to try to achieve these goals. Much of this will be centered around keywords and how effectively you have been able to target them.

- Do not only consider overall page ranking within search results for certain terms, but also look into how these higher, or lower, search results have impacted conversion rates for traffic and revenue.

- Consider the source of your incoming traffic as well as the keywords that have created this traffic through search queries. This will help you to more thoroughly focus your efforts on a smaller and more detailed set of keywords and phrases.

Chapter Nine

Paid Advertising and Sponsored Listings

What is paid advertising?

The methods that have been discussed so far within this book have been focused on creating organic traffic from unpaid search results. There are other ways to increase the visibility of your business within search results, and one of them includes that of paid advertising. Paid advertising is when a website pays for their listing to be put up when a number of specified search terms are used. In other cases, paid advertising can be found on other websites or blogs which are related to the business that is being promoted. There are a number of different ways that paid advertising is utilised within SEO, and it is a way to create stronger link building throughout the Internet.

What are sponsored listings?

Another method to increasing your SEO is through the use of sponsored listings. Sponsored listings are the highlighted links and advertisements that you normally see along the tops or sides of search engines. These listings often get the most attention as they are highlighted and likely to be in different colours. Taking advantage of these could be very beneficial.

You are able to pay the search engine, whether it be Google, Bing, Ask.com or Yahoo, a certain amount in order to come up as a sponsored listing when certain search terms are used. This allows you to be almost guaranteed that you will be listed first or second and above the rest of the results. The cost of sponsored listings can vary greatly by the terms that you focus on as well as the amount of times the link is seen by visitors.

How can paid advertising and sponsored listings improve SEO?

Investing in paid advertising as well as sponsored listings is a good way to boost your company's website SEO. It enables you to get a headstart on your competition and can be especially beneficial for businesses that are just starting. Because many new websites have trouble initially getting seen on search engines and being considered a trusted site, both paid advertising and sponsored listings will help them achieve the traffic necessary to gain exposure.

These tools can be used a number of ways and one of the benefits is that you are able to set up a paid advertising or listing sponsor campaign that lasts however long you need it to. This can help you cut down on the cost of advertising while still gaining the benefits of higher exposure and increased website traffic. Gaining visibility can turn into gaining a boost in sales and revenue.

What is pay per click?

Pay per click is a common type of advertising available on the Internet with the purpose of increasing traffic and website visitors. Within this model of advertising, the publisher will charge advertisers per the amount of times their advertisement is clicked. Publishers are usually the owners of website or search engine businesses. Pay per click advertising can be seen both on websites as well as on the sides of search results pages.

What services are available for paid advertising and sponsored listings?

There are a number of different services that provide tools and opportunities for paid advertising and sponsored links. Paid advertising can be found at a number of personally owned websites or organisation-owned websites. Sponsored listings are readily available through a number of search engine providers including Google, Yahoo!, and Microsoft.

Google AdWords

Google AdWords is the online advertising program created by Google. It works on the pay per click model and offers a large variety of options and customisation. It allows you to create the ads as well as decide upon any type of keywords or phrases that relate the best to your business. These ads will then appear on the Google search results as well as on other websites featuring the Google sponsored listings.

Yahoo! Search Marketing

Yahoo! has a Internet advertising program that can help your site utilise the sponsored listings that appear on the top and sides of every Yahoo! search. They provide you with a number of resources and a way to target your audience through keyword selection and ad specifications.

Microsoft adCenter

Microsoft adCenter is the paid advertising tool of Bing, and works similarly to both the Yahoo! and Google models. It allows you to target your main audience through keywords, as well as a number of training modules and advice on how to best optimize your site.

Summing Up

▨ Paid advertising and sponsored listings can be a vital part of boosting sales and website traffic.

▨ Sponsored listings are usually based on a pay per click model which allows advertisers to only pay for the amount of visibility the link gained.

▨ Yahoo!, Google and Bing all offer services for sponsored listings that would appear within the search terms relating to your site.

▨ Paid advertising is available at many different websites. Find websites within your industry that offer this option.

Glossary

Algorithm (Algo)
A program used by search engines to determine what pages to suggest for a given search query.

Alt text
A description of a graphic, which usually isn't displayed to the end user, unless the graphic is undeliverable, or a browser is used that doesn't display graphics. Alt text is important because search engines can't tell one picture from another. Alt text is the one place where it is acceptable for the spider to get different content than the human user, but only because the alt text is accessible to the user, and when properly used is an accurate description of the associated picture. Special web browsers for visually-challenged people rely on the alt text to make the content of graphics accessible to the users.

Analytics
A program which assists in gathering and analysing data about website usage. Google Analytics is a feature-rich, popular free analytics program.

Anchor text
The user-visible text of a link. Search engines use anchor text to indicate the relevancy of the referring site and of the link to the content on the landing page. Ideally all three will share some keywords in common.

Astroturfing (the opposite of full disclosure)
Attempting to advance a commercial or political agenda while pretending to be an impartial grass roots participant in a social group. Participating in a user forum with the secret purpose of branding, customer recruitment or public relations.

Authority (trust, link juice, Google juice)
The amount of trust that a site is credited with for a particular search query. Authority/trust is derived from related incoming links from other trusted sites.

Authority site

A website which has many incoming links from other related expert/hub sites. Because of this simultaneous citation from trusted hubs, an authority site usually has high trust, pagerank, and search results placement. Wikipedia, is an example of an authority site.

B2B

Business to business.

B2C

Business to consumer.

Backlink (inlink, incoming link)

Any link into a page or site from any other page or site.

Black hat

Search engine optimization tactics that are counter to best practices such as the Google Webmaster Guidelines.

Blog

A website which presents content in a more or less chronological series. Content may or may not be time-sensitive. Most blogs use a content management system such as WordPress rather than individually crafted WebPages. Because of this, the blogger can choose to concentrate on content creation instead of arcane code.

Bot (robot, spider, crawler)

A program which performs a task more or less autonomously. Search engines use bots to find and add web pages to their search indexes. Spammers often use bots to 'scrape' content for the purpose of plagiarising it for exploitation by the spammer.

Bounce rate

The percentage of users who enter a site and then leave it without viewing any other pages.

Bread crumbs

Website navigation in a horizontal bar above the main content which helps the user to understand where they are on the site and how to get back to the root areas.

Canonical issues (duplicate content)

Canon = legitimate or official version - It is often nearly impossible to avoid duplicate content, especially with CMSs like WordPress, but also due to the fact that www.site.com, site.com, and www.site.com/index.htm are supposedly seen as dupes by the SEs – although it's a bit hard to believe they aren't more sophisticated than that. However these issues can be dealt with effectively in several ways including – using the noindex meta tag in the non-canonical copies, and 301 server redirects to the canon.

Click fraud
Improper clicks on a PPC advertisement usually by the publisher or his minions for the purpose of undeserved profit. Click fraud is a huge issue for ad agencies like Google, because it lowers advertiser confidence that they will get fair value for their ad spend.

Cloak
The practice of delivering different content to the search engine spider than that seen by the human users. This black hat tactic is frowned upon by the search engines and carries a virtual death penalty of the site/domain being banned from the search engine results.

CMS (Content Management System)
Programs such as WordPress, which separate most of the mundane Webmaster tasks from content creation so that a publisher can be effective without acquiring or even understanding sophisticated coding skills if they so choose.

Code swapping (bait and switch)
Changing the content after high rankings are achieved.

Comment spam
Posting blog comments for the purpose of generating an inlink to another site. The reason many blogs use link condoms.

Content (text, copy)
The part of a web page that is intended to have value for and be of interest to the user. Advertising, navigation, branding and boilerplate are not usually considered to be content.

Contextual advertisement
Advertising which is related to the content.

Conversion (goal)
Achievement of a quantifiable goal on a website. Ad clicks, sign-ups, and sales are examples of conversions.

Conversion rate
Percentage of users who convert – see Conversion.

CPC – (cost per click)
The rate that is paid per click for a pay per click advertiser

CPM (cost per thousand impressions)
A statistical metric used to quantify the average value/cost of pay per click advertisements. M – from the Roman numeral for one thousand.

Crawler (bot, spider)
A program which moves through the World Wide Web or a website by way of the link structure to gather data.

Directory
A site devoted to directory pages. The Yahoo directory is an example.

Directory page
A page of links to related web pages.

Doorway (gateway)
A web page that is designed specifically to attract traffic from a search engine. A doorway page which redirects users (but not spiders) to another site or page is implementing cloaking.

Duplicate content
Content which is similar or identical to that found on another website or page. A site may not be penalised for serving duplicate content but it will receive little if any trust from the search engines compared to the content that the SE considers being the original.

e-commerce site
A website devoted to retail sales.

Feed

Content which is delivered to the user via special websites or programs such as news aggregators.

FFA (free for all)

A page or site with many outgoing links to unrelated websites, containing little, if any, unique content. Link farms are only intended for spiders, and have little, if any value to human users, and thus are ignored or penalised by the search engines.

Frames

A web page design where two or more documents appear on the same screen, each within its own frame. Frames are bad for SEO because spiders sometimes fail to correctly navigate them. Additionally, most users dislike frames because it is almost like having two tiny monitors neither of which shows a full page of information at one time.

Gateway page (doorway page)

A web page that is designed to attract traffic from a search engine and then redirect it to another site or page. A doorway page is not exactly the same as cloaking but the effect is the same in that users and search engines are served different content.

Gizmo (gadget, widget)

Small applications used on web pages to provide specific functions such as a hit counter or IP address display. Gizmos can make good link bait.

HTML (hyper text markup language)

Directives or 'markup' which are used to add formatting and web functionality to plain text for use on the Internet. HTML is the mother tongue of the search engines, and should generally be strictly and exclusively adhered to on web pages.

Impression (page view)

The event where a user views a web page one time.

Inbound link (inlink, incoming link)

Inbound links from related pages are the source of trust and PageRank.

Index

Noun - a database of web pages and their content used by the search engines.

Index

Verb - to add a web page to a search engine index.

Indexed pages

The pages on a site which have been indexed.

Inlink (incoming link, inbound link)

Inbound links from related pages are the source of trust and pagerank.

Keyword (key phrase)

The word or phrase that a user enters into a search engine.

Keyword cannibalization

The excessive reuse of the same keyword on too many web pages within the same site. This practice makes it difficult for the users and the search engines to determine which page is most relevant for the keyword.

Keyword density

The percentage of words on a web page which are a particular keyword. If this value is unnaturally high the page may be penalised.

Keyword research

The hard work of determining which keywords are appropriate for targeting.

Keyword spam (keyword stuffing)

Inappropriately high keyword density.

Keyword stuffing (keyword spam)

Inappropriately high keyword density.

Landing page

The page that a user lands on when they click on a link in an SERP.

Latent semantic indexing (LSI)

This mouthful just means that the search engines index commonly associated groups of words in a document. SEOs refer to these same groups of words as 'long tail searches'. The majority of searches consist of three or more words strung together. See also 'long tail'. The significance is that it might be almost impossible to rank well for 'mortgage', but fairly easy to rank for 'second mortgage to finance monster truck team'!

Link
An element on a web page that can be clicked on to cause the browser to jump to another page or another part of the current page.

Link bait
A web page with the designed purpose of attracting incoming links, often mostly via social media.

Link building
Actively cultivating incoming links to a site.

Link condom
Any of several methods used to avoid passing link love to another page, or to avoid possible detrimental results of endorsing a bad site by way of an outgoing link, or to discourage link spam in user generated content.

Link exchange
A reciprocal linking scheme often facilitated by a site devoted to directory pages. Link exchanges usually allow links to sites of low or no quality, and add no value themselves. Quality directories are usually human edited for quality assurance.

Link farm
A group of sites which all link to each other.

Link popularity
A measure of the value of a site based upon the number and quality of sites that link to it.

Link spam (comment spam)
Unwanted links such as those posted in user-generated content like blog comments.

Link text (anchor text)
The user-visible text of a link. Search engines use anchor text to indicate the relevancy of the referring site and link to the content on the landing page. Ideally all three will share some keywords in common.

Long tail

Longer more specific search queries that are often less targeted than shorter broad queries. For example a search for 'widgets' might be very broad while 'red widgets with reverse threads' would be a long tail search. A large percentage of all searches are long tail searches.

Mashup

A web page which consists primarily of single purpose software and other small programs (gizmos and gadgets) or possibly links to such programs. Mashups are quick and easy content to produce and are often popular with users, and can make good link bait. Tool collection pages are sometimes mashups.

Meta tags

Statements within the HEAD section of an HTML page which furnishes information about the page. Meta information may be in the SERPs but is not visible on the page. It is very important to have unique and accurate meta title and description tags, because they may be the information that the search engines rely upon the most to determine what the page is about. Also, they are the first impression that users get about your page within the SERPs.

Metric

A standard of measurement used by analytics programs.

Natural search results

The search engine results which are not sponsored, or paid for in any way.

Nofollow

A command found in either the HEAD section of a web page or within individual link code, which instructs robots to not follow either any links on the page or the specific link. A form of link condom.

Noindex

A command found in either the HEAD section of a web page or within individual link code, which instructs robots to not index the page or the specific link. A form of link condom.

Non-reciprocal link

If site A links to site B, but site B does not link back to site A, then the link is considered non-reciprocal. Search engines tend to give more value to non-reciprocal links than to reciprocal ones because they are less likely to be the result of collusion between sites.

Organic link

Organic links are those that are published only because the webmaster considers them to add value for users.

Outlink (outgoing link)

A HTML code on your site that allows visitors to your site to access other sites. Often just called a 'link'.

PageRank (PR)

A value between 0 and 1 assigned by the Google algorithm, which quantifies link popularity and trust among other (proprietary) factors. Often confused with Toolbar PageRank.

Pay for inclusion (PFI)

The practice of charging a fee to include a website in a search engine or directory. While quite common, usually what is technically paid for is more rapid consideration to avoid Google's prohibition on paid links.

Portal

A web service which offers a wide array of features to entice users to make the portal their 'home page' on the Web. iGoogle, Yahoo, and MSN are portals.

PPA (pay per action)

Very similar to pay per click except publishers only get paid when click throughs result in conversions.

PPC (pay per click)

A contextual advertisement scheme where advertisers pay ad agencies (such as Google) whenever a user clicks on their ad. Adwords is an example of PPC advertising.

Redirect

Any of several methods used to change the address of a landing page such as when a site is moved to a new domain, or in the case of a doorway.

Robots.txt

A file in the root directory of a website used to restrict and control the behaviour of search engine spiders.

ROI (return on investment)

One use of analytics software is to analyse and quantify return on investment, and thus cost/benefit of different schemes.

Sandbox

There has been debate and speculation that Google puts all new sites into a 'sandbox', preventing them from ranking well for anything until a set period of time has passed. The existence or exact behaviour of the sandbox is not universally accepted among SEOs.

Scrape

Copying content from a site, often facilitated by automated bots.

Search engine (SE)

A program, which searches a document or group of documents for relevant matches of a user's keyword phrase and returns a list of the most relevant matches. Internet search engines such as Google and Yahoo search the entire Internet for relevant matches.

Search engine spam

Pages created to cause search engines to deliver inappropriate or less relevant results. Search engine optimizers are sometimes unfairly perceived as search engine spammers. Of course in some cases they actually are.

SEM

Short for search engine marketing, SEM is often used to describe acts associated with researching, submitting and positioning a website within search engines to achieve maximum exposure of your website. SEM includes things such as search-engine optimization, paid listings and other search-engine-related services and functions that will increase exposure and traffic to your website.

SEO

Short for search engine optimization, the process of increasing the number of visitors to a website by achieving high ranks in the search results of a search engine. The higher a website ranks in the results of a search, the greater the chance that users will visit the site. It is common practice for Internet users to not click past the first few pages of search results, therefore high rank in SERPs is essential for obtaining traffic for a site. SEO helps to ensure that a site is accessible to a search engine and improves the chances that the site will be indexed and favourably ranked by the search engine.

SERP
Search engine results page.

Site map
A page or structured group of pages which link to every user-accessible page on a website, and hopefully improves site usability by clarifying the data structure of the site for the users. An XML sitemap is often kept in the root directory of a site just to help search engine spiders to find all of the site pages.

SMM (social media marketing)
Website or brand promotion through social media.

SMP (social media poisoning)
A term coined by Rand Fishkin – any of several (possibly illegal) black hat techniques designed to implicate a competitor as a spammer – For example, blog comment spamming in the name/brand of a competitor.

Social media
Various online technologies used by people to share information and perspectives. Blogs, Wikis, forums, social bookmarking, user reviews and rating sites (Digg, Reddit) are all examples of social media.

Spamdexing
Spamdexing, or search engine spamming, is the practice of deceptively modifying web pages to increase the chance of them being placed close to the beginning of search engine results, or to influence the category to which the page is assigned in a dishonest manner.

Spider (bot, crawler)
A specialised bot used by search engines to find and add web pages to their indexes.

Splash page

Often animated, graphics pages without significant textual content. Splash pages are intended to look flashy to humans, but without attention to SEO may look like dead ends to search engine spiders, which can only navigate through text links. Poorly executed splash pages may be bad for SEO and often a pain for users.

Static page

A web page without dynamic content or variables such as session IDs in the URL. Static pages are good for SEO work in that they are friendly to search engine spiders.

Stickiness

Mitigation of bounce rate. Website changes that entice users to stay on the site longer, and view more pages improve the sites 'stickiness'.

Supplemental index (supplemental results)

Pages with very low PageRank, which are still relevant to a search query, often appear in the SERPs with a label of supplemental result. Google's representatives say that this is not indicative of a penalty, only low PageRank.

Text link

A plain HTML link that does not involve graphic or special code such as Flash or Java script.

Time on page

The amount of time that a user spends on one page before clicking off. An indication of quality and relevance.

Toolbar pagerank (PR)

A value between 0 and 10 assigned by the Google algorithm, which quantifies page importance and is not the same as PageRank. Toolbar PageRank is only updated a few times a year, and is not a reliable indicator of current status. Often confused with PageRank.

Trust rank

A method of differentiating between valuable pages and spam by quantifying link relationships from trusted human evaluated seed pages.

URL

Uniform resource locator – AKA web address.

User generated content (UGC)

Social media, Wikis, Folksonomies and some blogs rely heavily on user generated content. One could say that Google is exploiting the entire Web as UGC for an advertising venue.

Help List

Bristol Web Design Company

T: 01179 58 54 50
M: 07851 23 37 91
Email: info@bristolwebdesignco.co.uk
Bristol Web Design Co offers cheap, affordable and professional website design and search engine optimisation (SEO) services throughout England and the UK.

Hobo Web Design

The Stables, 24 Patrick Street, Greenock, PA16 8NB. Scotland, UK
TEL 0845 094 0839
FAX 0845 868 8946
www.hobo-web.co.uk
We are the Hobo SEO company, based near Glasgow, in Scotland, in the UK. A professional SEO company, we use many SEO (search engine optimisation) techniques to get your site more traffic from search engines, with a particular focus and expertise on SEO for Google.co.uk, Bing.co.uk and Yahoo.co.uk.

Internet Marketing Scotland

Website Optimisation, The Pentagon Business Ctr. 36 Washington Street, Glasgow G3 8AZ, Scotland UK
Tel: 0141 353 9311
www.internetmarketingscotland.com

Red Evolution (Aberdeen) Ltd

Enterprise Business Centre, Admiral Court, Poynernook Rd, Aberdeen, AB11 5QX, Scotland, UK
Tel:+44 (0)1224 443551
E-mail: info@redevolution.com
www.redevolution.com

Aberdeen-based web company, and we help businesses like yours do more with the web by creating great websites and optimising them so they bring in business from search engines (SEO).

RFK Solutions

Bathgate Business Centre, 6 Whitburn Rd, Bathgate, West Lothian, EH48 1HH, Scotland, UK
Telephone :01506 637582
www.rfksolutions.co.uk
RFK Solutions offer new media business solutions which develop your brand and offer real results. We have been providing expert media services for over six years, in which time we have achieved incredible results for our clients which come from a mixture of industries and sectors

Search Dot Com

Conference Centre Offices, Brockhall Village, Old Langho, Lancashire, United Kingdom, BB6 8AY
Tel: 01254 454001 (UK 0044)
www.searchdotcom.co.uk
Backed by Paul Lynch who is one of the most well-respected SEO experts in the world. Search Dot Com Ltd, strives to offer only the highest quality SEO services.

The SEO Company

22 Bay View Court, Station Road, Lancaster, Lancashire, UK, LA1 5NL
Tel: +44 (0)1524 655 13
A Lancaster-based search engine optimisation specialist offering on-page SEO, link building, linkbaiting and social media optimisation services. We have been in business since 2006 and we have over 10 years' experience in the industry.
www.seoco.co.uk

Wildnet Technologies

Wildnet Technologies (P) Ltd, F-314, Sector-63, Noida (U.P.), India
Tel:+91-98102-92408
+91-98188-83238

+91-120-4533500
Email:leads@wildnettechnologies.com
www.wildnettechnologies.co.uk

References

SEOMoz [Online] Available at: http://www.seomoz.org/beginners-guide-to-seo [accessed March 10, 2012]

A Guide For the Independent Internet Publisher [Online] Available at:: http://www.websitepublisher.net/seo-guide/ [accessed March 10, 2012]

Google Search Engine Optimization Guide [Online] Available at: http://static.googleusercontent.com/external_content/untrusted_dlcp/www.google.com/en/us/webmasters/docs/search-engine-optimization-starter-guide.pdf [accessed March 10, 2012]

Available Titles Include ...

Allergies A Parent's Guide
ISBN 978-1-86144-064-8 £8.99

Autism A Parent's Guide
ISBN 978-1-86144-069-3 £8.99

Blood Pressure The Essential Guide
ISBN 978-1-86144-067-9 £8.99

Dyslexia and Other Learning Difficulties
A Parent's Guide ISBN 978-1-86144-042-6 £8.99

Bullying A Parent's Guide
ISBN 978-1-86144-044-0 £8.99

Epilepsy The Essential Guide
ISBN 978-1-86144-063-1 £8.99

Your First Pregnancy The Essential Guide
ISBN 978-1-86144-066-2 £8.99

Gap Years The Essential Guide
ISBN 978-1-86144-079-2 £8.99

Secondary School A Parent's Guide
ISBN 978-1-86144-093-8 £9.99

Primary School A Parent's Guide
ISBN 978-1-86144-088-4 £9.99

Applying to University The Essential Guide
ISBN 978-1-86144-052-5 £8.99

ADHD The Essential Guide
ISBN 978-1-86144-060-0 £8.99

Student Cookbook – Healthy Eating The Essential Guide
ISBN 978-1-86144-069-3 £8.99

Multiple Sclerosis The Essential Guide
ISBN 978-1-86144-086-0 £8.99

Coeliac Disease The Essential Guide
ISBN 978-1-86144-087-7 £9.99

Special Educational Needs A Parent's Guide
ISBN 978-1-86144-116-4 £9.99

The Pill An Essential Guide
ISBN 978-1-86144-058-7 £8.99

University A Survival Guide
ISBN 978-1-86144-072-3 £8.99

View the full range at **www.need2knowbooks.co.uk**.
To order our titles call **01733 898103**, email **sales@ n2kbooks.com** or visit the website. Selected ebooks available online.

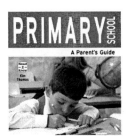
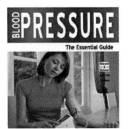
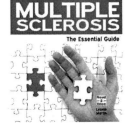

Need - 2 - Know, Remus House, Coltsfoot Drive, Peterborough, PE2 9BF